# NORTH CAROLINA GOVERNORS AND THEIR FINAL RESTING PLACES

# NORTH CAROLINA
# GOVERNORS
# AND THEIR FINAL
# RESTING PLACES

BY
ALDEN HOBBS

authorHOUSE®

*AuthorHouse™*
*1663 Liberty Drive*
*Bloomington, IN 47403*
*www.authorhouse.com*
*Phone: 1-800-839-8640*

*Published by AuthorHouse    08/16/2012*

*ISBN: 978-1-4772-5788-3 (sc)*
*ISBN: 978-1-4772-5789-0 (e)*

*Library of Congress Control Number: 2012914341*

*Any people depicted in stock imagery provided by Thinkstock are models, and such images are being used for illustrative purposes only.*
*Certain stock imagery © Thinkstock.*

*This book is printed on acid-free paper.*

# Contents

1. RICHARD CASWELL.................................................................. 12

2. ABNER NASH ...................................................................... 13

3. THOMAS BURKE ................................................................... 14

4. ALEXANDER MARTIN ............................................................ 15

5. SAMUEL JOHNSTON .............................................................. 16

6. RICHARD DOBBS SPAIGHT..................................................... 17

7. SAMUEL ASHE ..................................................................... 18

8. WILLIAM RICHARDSON DAVIE .............................................. 19

9. BENJAMIN WILLIAMS............................................................ 20

10. JAMES TURNER.................................................................... 21

11. NATHANIEL ALEXANDER...................................................... 22

12. DAVID STONE ..................................................................... 23

13. BENJAMIN SMITH................................................................ 24

14. WILLIAM HAWKINS ............................................................. 25

15. WILLIAM MILLER ................................................................ 26

16. JOHN BRANCH ................................................................... 27

17. JESSE FRANKLIN ................................................................. 28

18. GABRIEL HOLMES............................................................... 29

19. HUTCHINS GORDON BURTON.............................................. 30

20. JAMES IREDELL, JR.............................................................. 31

21. JOHN OWEN ...................................................................... 32

22. MONTFORT STOKES............................................................ 33

23. DAVID LOWRY SWAIN......................................................... 34

24. RICHARD DOBBS SPAIGHT, JR. ............................... 35

25. EDWARD BISHOP DUDLEY ..................................... 36

26. JOHN MOTLEY MOREHEAD...................................... 37

27. WILLIAM ALEXANDER GRAHAM ............................. 38

28. CHARLES MANLY ................................................... 39

29. DAVID SETTLE REID............................................... 40

30. WARREN WINSLOW ............................................... 41

31. THOMAS BRAGG .................................................... 42

32. JOHN WILLIS ELLIS................................................ 43

33. HENRY TOOLE CLARK ........................................... 44

34. ZEBULON BAIRD VANCE......................................... 45

35. WILLIAM WOODS HOLDEN .................................... 46

36. JONATHAN WORTH ............................................... 47

37. TOD ROBINSON CALDWELL.................................... 48

38. CURTIS HOOKS BROGDEN..................................... 49

39. THOMAS JORDAN JARVIS ...................................... 50

40. ALFRED MOORE SCALES ........................................ 51

41. DANIEL GOULD FOWLE .......................................... 52

42. THOMAS MICHAEL HOLT ...................................... 53

43. ELIAS CARR.......................................................... 54

44. DANIEL LINDSAY RUSSELL .................................... 55

45. CHARLES BRANTLEY AYCOCK ............................... 56

46. ROBERT BRODNAX GLENN .................................... 57

47. WILLIAM WALTON KITCHIN................................... 58

48. LOCKE CRAIG ...................................................... 59

49. THOMAS WALTER BICKETT ................................... 60

50. CAMERON MORRISON ........................................... 61

51. ANGUS WILTON MCLEAN....................................... 62

52. OLIVER MAXWELL GARDNER.................................. 63

53. JOHN C. B. EHRINGHAUS ........................................ 64

54. CLYDE ROARK HOEY............................................... 65

55. J. MELVILLE BROUGHTON ...................................... 66

56. ROBERT GREGG CHERRY......................................... 67

57. WILLIAM KERR SCOTT ........................................... 68

58. WILLIAM BRADLEY UMSTEAD............................... 69

59. LUTHER HARTWELL HODGES ............................... 70

60. JAMES TERRY SANFORD ......................................... 71

61. DANIEL KILLIAN MOORE......................................... 72

62. ROBERT WALTER SCOTT......................................... 73


63. CREDITS............................................................... 75

64. PHOTOGRAPHS ..................................................... 79

65. ABOUT THE AUTHOR ............................................ 81

THIS BOOK IS DEDICATED
TO MY FAMILY AND TO THE
PEOPLE OF CRAVEN COUNTY


BY

ALDEN HOBBS

There are different names referring to the areas of colonies in Virginia, North Carolina, and South Carolina. The Virginia Colony was also known as the Roanoke Colony. The Lords Proprietors was also the Proprietary Colony, which was the Governors of Albemarle Sound from 1664 to 1689.

It was changed to the Governors of Carolinas from 1689 to 1710. This was when Proprietors appointed one Governor of the entire Province, that was based in Charleston, to govern the South. They appointed a Deputy, known as Governor of "Ye Lands North and East of Cape Feare" to govern that area. In 1711, the creation of two separate governments were formed and there was a Governor from North Carolina and a Governor from South Carolina. This lasted twenty years until 1731, when it was known as the Royal Colony until 1775.

Samuel Stephens was Governor under the Southern Plantation and under the Lords Proprietors. George Burrington was Governor under the Lords Proprietors and under the Royal Governors.

Thomas Eastchurch and Henry Wilkinson never served as Governor. Their title was in name only. Thomas Cary refused to abandon the office of Governor to William Glover. Josiah Martin considered himself Governor throughout the Revolutionary War but left North Carolina in July, 1775.

During the appointments of North Carolina, the Governors from South Carolina were Thomas Smith, Joseph Blake, James Moore, Nathaniel Johnson, Edward Tynte, and Robert Gibbes.

# THE FIVE CHRONOLOGICAL STAGES OF N.C. GOVERNORS

## THE VIRGINIA COLONY

North Carolina governors have been part of the state since 1585 when Europe began their colonization period of the "New World." Queen Elizabeth commissioned Sir Walter Raleigh to establish a settlement that would secure England's claims to the territory. This new settlement would be called Virginia in honor of the virgin queen, Queen Elizabeth. This settlement included North Carolina and many other states.

## THE SOUTHERN PLANTATION

After the "Lost Colony" disappeared, the first successful English settlement was Jamestown. When South Virginia or the Roanoke Island area, which is now a part of North Carolina became more settled, it became known as the Southern Plantation. The governor of Virginia created a "Commander of the Southern Plantation." This was short lived because of the actions of the Virginia governor under the English Crown.

## THE LORDS PROPRIETORS

The Stuarts succeeded Queen Elizabeth as rulers of the throne and Charles II rewarded his loyal supporters by being made proprietors of Carolina, which reached from Virginia, through the Southern

Plantation, and to the northern part of Florida. The western boundary of Carolina was to be the "South Seas."

## THE ROYAL COLONY

Border disputes with Virginia, Indian wars, piracy at the hands of Blackbeard, the Proprietors had difficulty managing the colony. The British king recommended direct royal control of the colonies.

## THE STATE OF NORTH CAROLINA

Dissent within North Carolina grew under the rule of the king. Groups throughout North Carolina started to protest the dissatisfaction with royal government. In 1775, North Carolina patriots ran Josiah Martin, along with his family, out of North Carolina. He was the last royal governor of North Carolina.

North Carolina governors were chosen by the General Assembly from 1776 until the constitutional convention in 1835. After 1835, governors were elected by popular vote for 2 terms, and could be re-elected for another 2 years. In 1868, when North Carolina was readmitted to the Union, the new Constitution allowed for direct election of the governor for a single four year term. This remained true until 1977, when the 1971 Constitution was amended to allow a sitting governor to stand for re-election.

# CHRONOLOGY OF NORTH CAROLINA GOVERNORS

## ORIGINAL VIRGINIA COLONY

RALPH LANE, 1585-1586

JOHN WHITE, 1587

## COMMANDER OF THE SOUTHERN PLANTATION

SAMUEL STEPHENS, 1662-1664

## LORDS PROPRIETORS

WILLIAM DRUMMOND, 1664-1667

SAMUEL STEPHENS, 1667-1670

PETER CARTERET, 1670-1672

JOHN JENKINS, 1672-1675

THOMAS EASTCHURCH, 1675-1676

JOHN JENKINS, 1676-1677

THOMAS MILLER, 1677

SETH SOTHEL, 1678

JOHN HARVEY, 1679

HENRY WILKINSON, 1680

JOHN JENKINS, 1680-1681

SETH SOTHEL, 1682-1683

JOHN ARCHDALE, 1683-1686

SETH SOTHEL, 1686-1689

JOHN GIBBS, 1689-1690

PHILIP LUDWELL, 1690-1691

THOMAS JARVIS, 1691-1694

THOMAS HARVEY, 1694-1699

HENDERSON WALKER, 1699-1703

ROBERT DANIEL, 1703-1705

THOMAS CARY, 1705-1706

WILLIAM GLOVER, 1706-1708

THOMAS CARY, 1708-1711

EDWARD HYDE, 1711-1712

THOMAS POLLOCK, 1712-1714

CHARLES EDEN, 1714-1722

THOMAS POLLOCK, 1722

WILLIAM REED, 1722-1724

GEORGE BURRINGTON, 1724-1725

RICHARD EVERARD, 1725-1731

## ROYAL GOVERNORS

GEORGE BURRINGTON, 1731-1734

NATHANIEL RICE, 1734

GABRIEL JOHNSTON, 1734-1752

NATHANIEL RICE, 1752-1753

MATTHEW ROWAN, 1753-1754

ARTHUR DOBBS, 1754-1765

WILLIAM TRYON, 1765-1771

JAMES HASELL, 1771

JOSIAH MARTIN, 1771-1775

There are theories of several governors and where they are buried. I have traveled all over North Carolina and beyond to find all of the graves, but there are 8 governors that have not been located. Of the 8 governors, 4 have monuments in their honor near the location where they are thought to be buried, 2 are in unmarked graves in wooded areas, 1 is buried at sea off of Key West, Florida, and 1 is believed to be buried somewhere in Sparta, Georgia. This is a list of the names and where they are believed to be.

**Richard Caswell;**

It is believed that he died in Fayetteville, N.C. There was a funeral procession that left Fayetteville for Kinston, N.C. The actual burial is not known, but it is believed to be close to his monument in the Caswell Cemetery in Memorial Park.

**Alexander Martin;**

Alexander Martin was originally buried in a vault on the side of a hill where Jacobs Creek intersects with the Dan River on his Danbury Estate located near Madison, N.C. Worried about high water, he was relocated to the Settle Cemetery in Reidsville, N.C. There are no markers or head stone with his name on it, but there are several low spots in the cemetery where he is believed to be buried.

## James Turner;

Although the exact location of James Turner's grave is not clear, information given to me says he is buried near the Marmaduke area in Warren County. Old photos show depressions in the ground of 2 graves, one being Governor Turner's and the other being 1 of his 2 wives.

## David Stone;

It is not clear as to the exact location of David Stone's grave, he is believed to be buried in the Stone Family Burial Ground in Wake County. A monument was erected in his honor on his Restdale Plantation in Knightdale.

## Benjamin Smith;

It is believed that Benjamin Smith is buried in the Old Smithville Burying Ground in Southport, N.C. A monument has been placed there in his honor.

## William Hawkins;

A lot of time and research went into the location of his grave. After talking with several historical societies and chamber of commerce's in North Carolina and Georgia, the conclusion is he is buried in an unmarked grave in Sparta, Georgia.

**William Miller;**

William Miller was appointed by President John Quincy Adams as a diplomatic agent to Guatemala. He died of Yellow Fever in Key West, Florida en route to his new post and was buried at sea.

**Montfort Stokes;**

Montfort Stokes accepted an appointment by President Andrew Jackson as a member of the board of commissioners to deal with Indians in the West. He later became an agent for the Cherokees, Senecas, Shawnees, and Quapaws. He died shortly after that appointment. His grave is unmarked at Fort Gibson.

## There are 5 Governors that are still living;

**James Eubert Holshouser, Jr.**

Born—October 8, 1934—Boone, N.C.

68th Governor—1973-1977

Son of James and Virginia Holshouser

**James Baxter Hunt, Jr.**

Born—May 16, 1937—Wilson, N.C.

69th and 71st Governor—1977-1985, 1993-2001

Son of James and Elsie Hunt

**James Grubbs Martin**

Born—December 11, 1935—Savannah, Ga.

70th Governor—1985-1993

Son of Arthur and Mary Martin

**Michael Francis Easley**

Born—March 23, 1950—Rocky Mount, N.C.

72nd Governor—2001-2009

Son of Henry and Huldah Easley

**Beverly Eaves Perdue (Moore)**

Born—January 14, 1947—Grundy, Va.

73rd Governor—2009-2013

Daughter of Alfred and Irene Moore

Some of the dates on the early grave markers have been worn away by time. Usually it is the date when the governor is born.

Researchers from past and present use January 1 if the date is not known. I have also used this method.

If a date on a grave conflicts with the history books, I will use the date that appears most through my research.

Although rare, these problems did come up a few times during my research and fact finding.

# RICHARD CASWELL

AUGUST 3, 1729—NOVEMBER 10, 1789

1ST AND 5TH GOVERNOR OR NORTH
CAROLINA, 1776-1780, 1784-1787

CASWELL MEMORIAL PARK
KINSTON, N.C.

SON OF RICHARD AND CHRISTIAN CASWELL

# ABNER NASH

AUGUST 8, 1740—DECEMBER 2, 1786

2ND GOVERNOR OF NORTH CAROLINA

1780-1781

PEMBROKE PLANTATION CEMETERY

NEW BERN, N.C.

SON OF JOHN AND ANN NASH

# THOMAS BURKE

JANUARY 1, 1747—DECEMBER 2, 1783

3RD GOVERNOR OF NORTH CAROLINA
1781-1782

TYAQUIN PLANTATION
HILLSBOROUGH, N.C.

SON OF ULICK AND LETITIA BURKE

# ALEXANDER MARTIN

JANUARY 1, 1740—NOVEMBER 2, 1807

4TH AND 7TH GOVERNOR OF NORTH CAROLINA
1782-1785, 1789-1792

SETTLE FAMILY CEMETERY
REIDSVILLE, N.C.

SON OF HUGH AND JANE MARTIN

# SAMUEL JOHNSTON

DECEMBER 15, 1733—AUGUST 17, 1816

6TH GOVERNOR OF NORTH CAROLINA
1787-1789

JOHNSTON BURIAL GROUND
EDENTON, N.C.

SON OF SAMUEL AND HELEN JOHNSTON

# RICHARD DOBBS SPAIGHT

MARCH 25, 1758—SEPTEMBER 6, 1802

8TH GOVERNOR OF NORTH CAROLINA
1792-1795

CLERMONT CEMETERY
NEW BERN, N.C.

SON OF RICHARD AND ELIZABETH SPAIGHT

# SAMUEL ASHE

MARCH 24, 1725—FEBRUARY 13, 1813

9TH GOVERNOR OF NORTH CAROLINA
1795-1798

ASHE CEMETERY
BURGAW, N.C.

SON OF JOHN AND ELIZABETH ASHE

# WILLIAM RICHARDSON DAVIE

JUNE 22, 1756—NOVEMBER 5, 1820

10TH GOVERNOR OF NORTH CAROLINA
1798-1799

OLD WAXHAW PRESBYTERIAN CHURCH
LANCASTER, S.C.

SON OF ARCHIBALD AND MARY DAVIE

# BENJAMIN WILLIAMS

JANUARY 1, 1751—JULY 20, 1814

11TH AND 14TH GOVERNOR OF NORTH
CAROLINA, 1799-1802, 1807-1808

HOUSE IN THE HORSESHOE
SANFORD, N.C.

SON OF JOHN AND FEREBEE WILLIAMS

# JAMES TURNER

DECEMBER 20, 1766—JANUARY 15, 1824

12TH GOVERNOR OF NORTH CAROLINA

1802-1805

Grave of Former N. C. Governor, Senator

FISHING CREEK PLANTATION

MARMADUKE—INEZ AREA

WARREN COUNTY, N.C.

SON OF THOMAS AND REBECCA TURNER

# NATHANIEL ALEXANDER

MARCH 5, 1756—MARCH 7, 1808

13TH GOVERNOR OF NORTH CAROLINA
1805-1807

OLD SETTLERS CEMETERY
CHARLOTTE, N.C.

SON OF MOSES AND SARAH ALEXANDER

# DAVID STONE

FEBRUARY 17, 1770—OCTOBER 7, 1818

15TH GOVERNOR OF NORTH CAROLINA
1808-1810

RESTDALE PLANTATION
KNIGHTDALE, N.C.

SON OF ZEDEKIAH AND ELIZABETH STONE

# BENJAMIN SMITH

JANUARY 10, 1756—JANUARY 26, 1826

16TH GOVERNOR OF NORTH CAROLINA
1810-1811

OLD SMITHVILLE CEMETERY
SOUTHPORT, N.C.

SON OF THOMAS AND SARAH SMITH

# WILLIAM HAWKINS

OCTOBER 20, 1777—MAY 17, 1819

17TH GOVERNOR OF NORTH CAROLINA

1811-1814

UNMARKED GRAVE

SPARTA, GEORGIA

SON OF PHILEMON AND LUCY HAWKINS

# WILLIAM MILLER

JANUARY 1, 1770—DECEMBER 10, 1825

18TH GOVERNOR OF NORTH CAROLINA
1814-1817

BURIED AT SEA
ATLANTIC OCEAN

SON OF THOMAS MILLER AND MISS LOVE

# JOHN BRANCH

NOVEMBER 4, 1782—JANUARY 4, 1863

19TH GOVERNOR OF NORTH CAROLINA
1817-1820

ELMWOOD CEMETERY
ENFIELD, N.C.

SON OF JOHN AND REBECCA BRANCH

# JESSE FRANKLIN

MARCH 24, 1760—AUGUST 31, 1823

20TH GOVERNOR OF NORTH CAROLINA

1820-1821

GUILFORD NATIONAL PARK

GREENSBORO, N.C.

SON OF BERNARD AND MARY FRANKLIN

# GABRIEL HOLMES

JANUARY 1, 1769—SEPTEMBER 26, 1829

21ST GOVERNOR OF NORTH CAROLINA

1821-1824

JOHN SAMPSON CEMETERY

CLINTON, N.C.

SON OF GABRIEL AND MARY HOLMES

# HUTCHINS GORDON BURTON

JANUARY 1, 1774—APRIL 21, 1836

22ND GOVERNOR OF NORTH CAROLINA

1824-1827

UNITY PRESBYTERIAN CHURCH

DENVER, N.C.

SON OF JOHN AND MARY BURTON

# JAMES IREDELL, JR.

NOVEMBER 2, 1788—APRIL 13, 1853

23RD GOVERNOR OF NORTH CAROLINA
1827-1828

HAYES PLANTATION
EDENTON, N.C.

SON OF JAMES AND HANNAH IREDELL

# JOHN OWEN

AUGUST 1, 1787—OCTOBER 9, 1841

24TH GOVERNOR OF NORTH CAROLINA
1828-1830

ST. BARTHOLOMEW EPISCOPAL CHURCH
PITTSBORO. N.C.

SON OF THOMAS AND ELEANOR OWEN

# MONTFORT STOKES

MARCH 12, 1762—NOVEMBER 4, 1842

25TH GOVERNOR OF NORTH CAROLINA
1830-1832

FORT GIBSON NATIONAL CEMETERY
FORT GIBSON, OK.

SON OF DAVID AND SARAH STOKES

# DAVID LOWRY SWAIN

JANUARY 4, 1801—AUGUST 27, 1868

26TH GOVERNOR OF NORTH CAROLINA
1832-1835

OAKWOOD CEMETERY
RALEIGH, N.C.

SON OF GEORGE AND CAROLINE SWAIN

# RICHARD DOBBS SPAIGHT, JR.

JANUARY 1, 1796—NOVEMBER 2, 1850

27TH GOVERNOR OF NORTH CAROLINA

1835-1836

CLERMONT CEMETERY

NEW BERN, N.C.

SON OF RICHARD AND MARY SPAIGHT

# EDWARD BISHOP DUDLEY

DECEMBER 15, 1789—OCTOBER 30, 1855

28TH GOVERNOR OF NORTH CAROLINA
1836-1841

OAKDALE CEMETERY
WILMINGTON, N.C.

SON OF CHRISTOPHER AND MARGARET DUDLEY

# JOHN MOTLEY MOREHEAD

JULY 4, 1796—AUGUST 27, 1866

29TH GOVERNOR OF NORTH CAROLINA

1841-1845

OLD 1ST PRESBYTERIAN CHURCH

GREENSBORO, N.C.

SON OF JOHN AND OBEDIENCE MOREHEAD

# WILLIAM ALEXANDER GRAHAM

SEPTEMBER 5, 1804—AUGUST 11, 1875

30TH GOVERNOR OF NORTH CAROLINA
1845-1849

HILLSBOROUGH PRESBYTERIAN CHURCH
HILLSBOROUGH, N.C.
SON OF JOSEPH AND ISABELLA GRAHAM

# CHARLES MANLY

MAY 13, 1795—MAY 1, 1871

31ST GOVERNOR OF NORTH CAROLINA
1849-1850

CITY CEMETERY
RALEIGH, N.C.

SON OF BASIL AND ELIZABETH MANLY

# DAVID SETTLE REID

APRIL 19, 1813—JUNE 18, 1891

32ND GOVERNOR OF NORTH CAROLINA
1851-1854

GREENVIEW CEMETERY
REIDSVILLE, N.C.

SON OF REUBEN AND ELIZABETH REID

# WARREN WINSLOW

JANUARY 1, 1810—AUGUST 16, 1862

33RD GOVERNOR OF NORTH CAROLINA
1854-1855

CROSS CREEK CEMETERY
FAYETTEVILLE, N.C.

SON OF JOHN AND CAROLINE WINSLOW

# THOMAS BRAGG

NOVEMBER 9, 1810—JANUARY 21, 1872

34TH GOVERNOR OF NORTH CAROLINA
1855-1859

OAKWOOD CEMETERY
RALEIGH, N.C.

SON OF THOMAS AND MARGARET BRAGG

# JOHN WILLIS ELLIS

NOVEMBER 23, 1820—JULY 7, 1861

35TH GOVERNOR OF NORTH CAROLINA
1859-1861

OLD ENGLISH CEMETERY
SALISBURY, N.C.

SON OF ANDERSON AND JUDITH ELLIS

# HENRY TOOLE CLARK

FEBRUARY 7, 1808—APRIL 14, 1874

36TH GOVERNOR OF NORTH CAROLINA

1861-1862

CALVARY CHURCHYARD

TARBORO, N.C.

SON OF JAMES AND ARABELLA CLARK

# ZEBULON BAIRD VANCE

MAY 13, 1830—APRIL 14, 1894

37TH AND 43RD GOVERNOR OF NORTH CAROLINA,
1862-1865, 1877-1879

RIVERSIDE CEMETERY
ASHEVILLE, N.C.

SON OF DAVID AND MIRA VANCE

# WILLIAM WOODS HOLDEN

## NOVEMBER 24, 1818—MARCH 1, 1892

## 38TH AND 40TH GOVERNOR OF NORTH CAROLINA, 1865, 1868-1870

### OAKWOOD CEMETERY
### RALEIGH, N.C.

### SON OF THOMAS HOLDEN AND PRISCILLA WOODS

# JONATHAN WORTH

NOVEMBER 18, 1802—SEPTEMBER 5, 1869

39TH GOVERNOR OF NORTH CAROLINA
1865-1868

OAKWOOD CEMETERY

RALEIGH, N.C.

SON OF DAVID AND EUNICE WORTH

# TOD ROBINSON CALDWELL

### FEBRUARY 19, 1818—JULY 11, 1874

### 41ST GOVERNOR OF NORTH CAROLINA
### 1870-1874

### FOREST HILL CEMETERY
### MORGANTON, N.C.

### SON OF JOHN AND HANNAH CALDWELL

# CURTIS HOOKS BROGDEN

NOVEMBER 6, 1816—JANUARY 5, 1901

42ND GOVERNOR OF NORTH CAROLINA

1874-1877

WILLOWDALE CEMETERY

GOLDSBORO, N.C.

SON OF PIERCE AND AMY BROGDEN

# THOMAS JORDAN JARVIS

JANUARY 18, 1836—JUNE 17, 1915

44TH GOVERNOR OF NORTH CAROLINA
1879-1885

CHERRY HILL CEMETERY
GREENVILLE, N.C.

SON OF BANNISTER AND ELIZABETH JARVIS

# ALFRED MOORE SCALES

NOVEMBER 26, 1827—FEBRUARY 9, 1892

45TH GOVERNOR OF NORTH CAROLINA
1885-1889

GREEN HILL CEMETERY
GREENSBORO, N.C.

SON OF ROBERT AND JANE SCALES

# DANIEL GOULD FOWLE

MARCH 13, 1831—APRIL 7, 1891

46TH GOVERNOR OF NORTH CAROLINA
1889-1891

OAKWOOD CEMETERY
RALEIGH, N.C.

SON OF SAMUEL AND MARTHA FOWLE

# THOMAS MICHAEL HOLT

JULY 15, 1831—APRIL 11, 1896

47TH GOVERNOR OF NORTH CAROLINA

1891-1893

LINWOOD CEMETERY

GRAHAM, N.C.

SON OF EDWIN AND EMILY HOLT

# ELIAS CARR

FEBRUARY 25, 1839—JULY 22, 1900

48TH GOVERNOR OF NORTH CAROLINA

1893-1897

CARR FAMILY CEMETERY

MACCLESFIELD, N.C.

SON OF JONAS AND ELIZABETH CARR

# DANIEL LINDSAY RUSSELL

AUGUST 7, 1845—MAY 14, 1908

49TH GOVERNOR OF NORTH CAROLINA
1897-1901

D.W. SANDERS/HICKORY HILLS CEMETERY
BELGRADE, N.C.

SON OF DANIEL AND ELIZABETH RUSSELL

# CHARLES BRANTLEY AYCOCK

NOVEMBER 1, 1859—APRIL 4, 1912

50TH GOVERNOR OF NORTH CAROLINA
1901-1905

OAKWOOD CEMETERY
RALEIGH, N.C.

SON OF BENJAMIN AND SERENA AYCOCK

# ROBERT BRODNAX GLENN

AUGUST 11, 1854—MAY 16, 1920

51ST GOVERNOR OF NORTH CAROLINA
1905-1909

SALEM CEMETERY
WINSTON-SALEM, N.C.

SON OF CHALMERS AND ANNIE GLENN

# WILLIAM WALTON KITCHIN

OCTOBER 9, 1866—NOVEMBER 9, 1924

52ND GOVERNOR OF NORTH CAROLINA

1909-1913

BAPTIST CEMETERY

SCOTLAND NECK, N.C.

SON OF WILLIAM AND MARIE KITCHIN

# LOCKE CRAIG

AUGUST 16, 1860—JUNE 9, 1924

53RD GOVERNOR OF NORTH CAROLINA

1913-1917

RIVERSIDE CEMETERY

ASHEVILLE, N.C.

SON OF ANDREW AND CLARISSA CRAIG

# THOMAS WALTER BICKETT

FEBRUARY 28, 1869—DECEMBER 28, 1921

54TH GOVERNOR OF NORTH CAROLINA

1917-1921

OAKWOOD CEMETERY

LOUISBURG, N.C.

SON OF THOMAS AND MARY BICKETT

# CAMERON MORRISON

## OCTOBER 5, 1869—AUGUST 20, 1953

## 55TH GOVERNOR OF NORTH CAROLINA
## 1921-1925

## ELMWOOD CEMETERY
## CHARLOTTE, N.C.

## SON OF DANIEL AND MARTHA MORRISON

# ANGUS WILTON MCLEAN

APRIL 20, 1870—JUNE 21, 1935

56TH GOVERNOR OF NORTH CAROLINA
1925-1929

MEADOWBROOK CEMETERY
LUMBERTON, N.C.

SON OF ARCHIBALD AND CAROLINE MCLEAN

# OLIVER MAXWELL GARDNER

MARCH 22, 1882—FEBRUARY 6, 1947

57TH GOVERNOR OF NORTH CAROLINA

1929-1933

SUNSET CEMETERY

SHELBY, N.C.

SON OF OLIVER AND MARGARET GARDNER

# JOHN C. B. EHRINGHAUS

FEBRUARY 5, 1882—JULY 31, 1949

58TH GOVERNOR OF NORTH CAROLINA

1933-1937

EPISCOPAL CEMETERY

ELIZABETH CITY, N.C.

SON OF ERSKINE AND CATHERINE EHRINGHAUS

# CLYDE ROARK HOEY

DECEMBER 11, 1877—MAY 12, 1954

59TH GOVERNOR OF NORTH CAROLINA
1937-1941

SUNSET CEMETERY
SHELBY, N.C.

SON OF SAMUEL AND MARY HOEY

# J. MELVILLE BROUGHTON

NOVEMBER 17, 1888—MARCH 6, 1949

60TH GOVERNOR OF NORTH CAROLINA
1941-1945

MONTLAWN CEMETERY
RALEIGH, N.C.

SON OF JOSEPH AND SALLIE BROUGHTON

# ROBERT GREGG CHERRY

OCTOBER 17, 1891—JUNE 25, 1957

61ST GOVERNOR OF NORTH CAROLINA

1945-1949

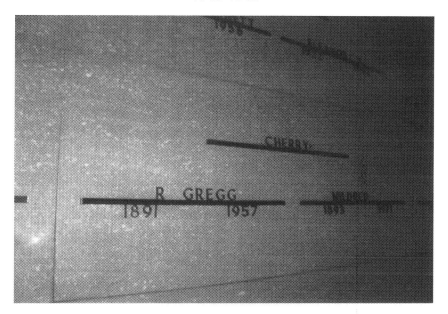

GASTON MEMORIAL PARK

GASTONIA, N.C.

SON OF LAFAYETTE AND HATTIE CHERRY

# WILLIAM KERR SCOTT

APRIL 17, 1896—APRIL 16, 1958

62ND GOVERNOR OF NORTH CAROLINA
1949-1953

HAWFIELDS PRESBYTERIAN CHURCH
MEBANE, N.C.

SON OF ROBERT AND ELIZABETH SCOTT

# WILLIAM BRADLEY UMSTEAD

MAY 13, 1895—NOVEMBER 7, 1954

63RD GOVERNOR OF NORTH CAROLINA

1953-1954

MT. TABOR METHODIST CHURCH

BAHAMA, N.C.

SON OF JOHN AND LULIE UMSTEAD

# LUTHER HARTWELL HODGES

MARCH 9, 1898—OCTOBER 6, 1974

64TH GOVERNOR OF NORTH CAROLINA

1954-1961

OVERLOOK CEMETERY

EDEN, N.C.

SON OF JOHN AND LOVICIA HODGES

# JAMES TERRY SANFORD

## AUGUST 20, 1917—APRIL 18, 1998

## 65TH GOVERNOR OF NORTH CAROLINA
### 1961-1965

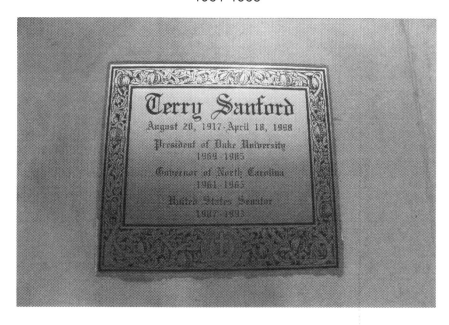

## DUKE CHAPEL
## DURHAM, N.C.

## SON OF CECIL AND ELIZABETH SANFORD

# DANIEL KILLIAN MOORE

APRIL 2, 1906—SEPTEMBER 7, 1986

66TH GOVERNOR OF NORTH CAROLINA

1965-1969

OAKWOOD CEMETERY

RALEIGH, N.C.

SON OF FRED AND LELA MOORE

# ROBERT WALTER SCOTT

JUNE 13, 1929—JANUARY 23, 2009

67TH GOVERNOR OF NORTH CAROLINA

1969-1973

HAWFIELDS PRESBYTERIAN CHURCH

MEBANE, N.C.

SON OF WILLIAM AND MARY SCOTT

# CREDITS

Monika Fleming, Edgecombe Community College, Tarboro,N.C.
ELIAS CARR, HENRY TOOLE CLARK

Stan Little, N.C. Department of Cultural Resources,
Greenville,N.C.

Danny Morgan, Park operations supervisor, Cemeteries and
Pullen Park,
Raleigh,N.C.
CHARLES MANLY

Paula M. Peters, Administrative Asst.,
Clinton, Sampson County C of C
Clinton, N.C.
GABRIEL HOLMES

Eleanor Bradshaw, Sampson County Register of Deeds
Clinton, N.C.
GABRIEL HOLMES

Joel Rose, Sampson County Historical Society,
Clinton,N.C.,
Nadine Strickland Historical Society

Karen-Marie Allen, Olivia Raney Local History Library
Raleigh, N.C.

Michael Hill, N.C. Office of Archives and History,
Research Branch Supervisor,
N.C. Highway Historical Marker Program,
Author—the Governors of N.C.

Rick Joslyn, President Sparta, Ga. Historical Society
WILLIAM HAWKINS

Charles Rodenbough, author—Alexander Martin

Jeri Waldruss (Martin), Historian Madison, N.C.
Lindley Butler (Martin), Historian, Teacher

Charles Holtzclaw, Director Sunset Cemetery,
Shelby, N.C.
CLYDE ROARK HOEY, OLIVER MAX GARDNER

Jay Stevens, Warren County
Cynthia Haiphcock, Warren County

Edith Batson, Burgaw, N.C., Post Staff Writer, Pender Post
SAMUEL ASHE

Lancaster County,S.C. Chamber of Commerce
WILLIAM RICHARDSON DAVIE

Craven Regional Library
Kellenberger Room


The Governors of North Carolina edited by Michael Hill


North Carolina Governors
By Beth G. Crabtree www.ncgovernors.state politicalgraveyards.
com findagrave.com www.northcarolinahistory.org

# PHOTOGRAPHS

Lancaster County, S.C. Chamber of Commerce;
William Richardson Davie

Warren County Newspaper;
James Turner

Alden Hobbs III;
Benjamin Smith

Images of Sparta, Ga.;
William Hawkins

Rachel C. Hobbs;
William Miller

Images of Fort Gibson National Cemetery;
Montfort Stokes

L. Mackenzie Cover;
Zebulon Baird Vance
Tod Robinson Caldwell
Locke Craig

Special thanks go to several people for helping in their own way with this book.

Karen C. Hobbs

Alden Hobbs, III

Rachel C. Hobbs

Martha Ann Hobbs

Ann H. Cover

L. Mackenzie Cover

Charles Rodenbough

Cynthia Haiphcock

Edith Batson

Joel Rose

Knightdale Fire Dept.

Ladies of the Lancaster Chamber

The Graphics Shack

# About the Author

Born in 1961, Alden Hobbs, Jr. grew up in Kinston, which is located in Eastern North Carolina. After graduating from Arendell Parrott Academy in 1979, he went to Louisburg College and East Carolina University. After 10 years in the tobacco business, he changed careers and is now working for the Postal Service. He now lives in New Bern, N.C. with his wife, Karen and 2 children, Alden, III and Rachel. In researching this book, he would get most of his pictures when he traveled with his family to soccer games and tournaments throughout the state. It has taken almost 2 years to locate all of the graves in this book. Hope you can appreciate this book and are able to learn more about the Governors of North Carolina.

Alden Hobbs, Jr. has also written Mountain Dew, Minges, and Me.